D0759024

Lindsey Vonn

By Sarah Dann

Crabtree Publishing Company

www.crabtreebooks.com

Crabtree Publishing Company

www.crabtreebooks.com

Author: Sarah Dann
Publishing plan research and development:
 Reagan Miller
Editors: Molly Aloian, Crystal Sikkens
Proofreader and indexer: Wendy Scavuzzo
Photo research: Crystal Sikkens
Designer: Ken Wright
Production coordinator and prepress
 technician: Ken Wright
Print coordinator: Margaret Amy Salter

Photographs:
Associated Press: pages 9, 16, 18
Getty Images: Rob Carr/Staff: page 6;
 Sports Illustrated: pages 8, 20, 27; Brian
 Bahr/Staff: page 10/ AFP: pages 11, 13, 14,
 15; Agence Zoom/Stringer: page 12; Jeff
 Vinnick/Stringer: page 17
Keystone Press: zumapress.com: pages 4, 7, 22;
 wenn.com: page 23; BEImages: page 28
Shutterstock: B.Stefanov: cover, pages 5, 26;
 Mitch Gunn: pages 1, 19; Helga Esteb:
 page 21; s_bukley: pages 24, 25

Every effort has been made to trace copyright holders and to obtain their permission for use of copyright material. The authors and publishers would be pleased to rectify any error or omission in future editions. All the Internet addresses given in this book were correct at the time of going to press. The author and publishers regret any inconvenience caused if addresses have changed or sites have ceased to exist, but can accept no responsibility for any such changes.

Library and Archives Canada Cataloguing in Publication

Dann, Sarah, 1970-, author
    Lindsey Vonn / Sarah Dann.

(Superstars!)
Includes index.
Issued in print and electronic formats.
ISBN 978-0-7787-0025-8 (bound).--ISBN 978-0-7787-0067-8
(pbk).--ISBN 978-1-4271-9385-8 (pdf).--ISBN 978-1-4271-9379-7
(html)

    1. Vonn, Lindsey--Juvenile literature. 2. Skiers--United
States--Biography--Juvenile literature. I. Title. II. Series:
Superstars! (St. Catharines, Ont.)

GV854.2.V66D35 2013   j796.93'5092   C2013-905225-9
                                                 C2013-905226-7

Library of Congress Cataloging-in-Publication Data

CIP available at Library of Congress

Crabtree Publishing Company

Printed in Canada/092013/BF20130815

www.crabtreebooks.com   1-800-387-7650

Published in Canada
Crabtree Publishing
616 Welland Ave.
St. Catharines, ON
L2M 5V6

Published in the United States
Crabtree Publishing
PMB 59051
350 Fifth Avenue, 59th Floor
New York, New York 10118

Published in the United Kingdom
Crabtree Publishing
Maritime House
Basin Road North, Hove
BN41 1WR

Published in Australia
Crabtree Publishing
3 Charles Street
Coburg North
VIC 3058

CONTENTS

Words that are defined in the glossary are in
bold type the first time they appear in the text.

Meet Lindsey Vonn

Superstar athlete Lindsey Vonn is one of the most accomplished **downhill** skiers of our time. By the time she was only 18 years old, Lindsey had won three World Cup downhill titles! Lindsey is now in her early 30s, and she has won 59 World Cup races. Lindsey shows no signs of slowing down and this number will no doubt climb as she continues to make her way down the slopes.

Amazing American

Lindsey is only the second woman in American history to win the **Overall World Cup Championship** and has done so four times to date! She is also considered the most successful skier on the U.S. Ski Team. She was the first American woman to win the Olympic gold medal in downhill skiing and has also won Olympic bronze for the United States.

Lindsey Vonn has won 17 Crystal Globe trophies for winning World Cup skiing titles.

4

Tough Competitor

Lindsey is known for being a fierce competitor and has not let injuries hold her back from becoming a champion. She is known for her determination, **perseverance**, and for her ability to come back after crashes and injuries. Lindsey says, "The one thing I've learned in life is that when you fall, you just get back up." Lindsey amazes fans and fellow athletes with her speed and aggression on the slopes and her winning personality off the slopes.

SEEN ON TV

Lindsey's popularity has landed her on several television programs such as *The Today Show, Late Show with David Letterman,* and *The Ellen DeGeneres Show*.

Lindsey's typical speed and aggressive approach won her first place at this World Cup **Super-G** race in Bansko, Bulgaria, in February 2012.

5

A Ski Star Is Born

On October 18, 1984, Lindsey Caroline Kildow was born in St. Paul, Minnesota, to parents Linda and Alan Kildow. St. Paul, is not known for being a ski town, but Lindsey had skiing in her blood— both her father and grandfather were competitive skiers and this tradition would live on through Lindsey. Lindsey's father had her up on skis when she was three.

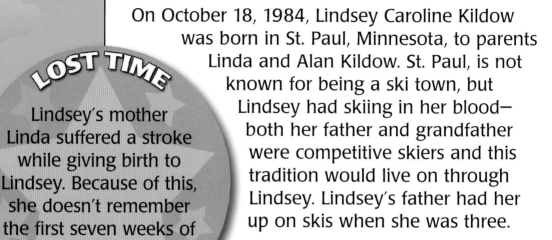

LOST TIME

Lindsey's mother Linda suffered a stroke while giving birth to Lindsey. Because of this, she doesn't remember the first seven weeks of Lindsey's life.

Trained to Win

At a very young age, Lindsey was put into a famous training program run by a well-known ski coach named Erich Sailer. Sailer's program ran on the ski hills near Minnesota. He has trained many of the U.S. Ski Team's top competitors. His **prestigious** program is known for turning junior ski racers into champions by teaching them the latest ski techniques. According to Sailer, Lindsey's father pushed her very hard. As Lindsey grew up, her relationship with her father became strained.

Lindsey cut ties with her father for many years, but they have since reconnected.

Young Child with Talent

Lindsey's skiing skills were apparent early on. At seven years old, Lindsey began racing and, by nine years old, she was competing in international skiing events. When she was 11 years old, Lindsey and her mother moved to Vail, Colorado, so she could train at Ski Club Vail, a top-rated winter-sports academy. Her mother homeschooled her through the winter months while her father, two brothers, and two sisters stayed in Minnesota. In the late 1990s, the entire family decided to relocate to Vail.

SKIING IN THE FAMILY

Lindsey's father Alan was a junior ski racer. He won a national junior title in 1970 when he was 17 years old. One year later, Alan seriously injured his knee and was unable to continue skiing.

Lindsey has four younger siblings—sister Karin, and triplets Reed, Dylan, and Laura (shown below left).

7

Early Influences

When Lindsey was ten years old, she met the Olympic medalist and World Cup champion Picabo Street at an autograph signing at Pierce Skate & Ski in Minneapolis, Minnesota. Meeting the successful American skier made a lasting impression on Lindsey, and the two would meet again as Lindsey's career progressed.

American Olympic skier and medalist Picabo Street

Big Win in Italy

Lindsey's hard work and training began to pay off in 1999. She became the first American ever to win an important race in Italy called the Trofeo Topolino. Known to skiers as "the junior Junior Worlds," this race is for skiers aged 11−14. Lindsey's win put her on the map as one of the best junior racers in the world. Many girls who have won this race have gone on to win the overall World Cup Championship and, for Lindsey, this was a sign of things to come.

Fighting Forward

At age 15, Lindsey started competing in International Ski Federation races. These earned her points toward joining the U.S. Olympic Ski Team. Lindsey finished on the **podium** several times and earned her first win in 2001. That same year, she won bronze in the **combined** at the U.S. National Championships. She also competed in her first-ever World Cup event and finished 26th in the Super-G at Val d'Isere, a famous ski hill in France.

Learning Along the Way

To keep up with her high school studies while training and racing, Lindsey completed courses through the University of Missouri's online High School Program. The online program allowed Lindsey to learn the subjects and complete assignments without taking too much time away from the slopes.

Lindsey has become friends with many of the skiers she competes with, but that hasn't made her any less competitive!

Joining Her Hero

When Lindsey was 16, she fought her way through the ranks and secured a top spot on the U.S. Ski Team. Also on the team that year was someone Lindsey looked up to—Picabo Street. Picabo remembers Lindsey standing out because she paid close attention to everything Picabo said. When she saw Lindsey ski, Picabo was impressed with Lindsey's technique and she noticed how well Lindsey followed the **fall line** of the hill. The two became friends and, although Picabo retired soon after their year together on the team, she has continued to mentor, or teach and give tips to, Lindsey throughout her career.

At age 17, Lindsey poses for her U.S. Ski Team portrait.

Early Olympic Performances

At age 17, Lindsey qualified for and competed in the 2002 Winter Olympics in Salt Lake City, Utah. She placed sixth in the combined event. That was the highest placing by an American skier that year, so the win was a huge accomplishment for Lindsey at such a young age. Sadly, Lindsey was also dealing with personal troubles around that time as her parents were getting a divorce.

KEEPING UP

As a teenager, Lindsey went for a mountain bike ride with her friend, a fellow skier named Julia Mancuso. She couldn't keep up and decided she needed to add cycling to her training routine.

Lindsey races here in the 2002 Olympic Games—her first Olympic competition.

11

World Traveler

Lindsey was now traveling all over the world for races. Not being home much made it a little easier to deal with the fact that her parents were no longer together. Her schedule was packed with races and training in the off-season. Lindsey says that she didn't have a typical life growing up—no sleepovers, parties, or proms. Her life revolved around skiing and traveling, and her friends largely lived within the ski world.

Lindsey (right) was very excited about her first trip to the podium at a World Cup event. She won third place in Cortina d'Ampezzo, Italy.

Junior Star

Lindsey continued her rise through 2003 and 2004 when she competed in several junior competitions. In 2003, Lindsey captured a silver medal at the Junior World Championships, and silver and bronze medals at the U.S. Nationals. In 2004, she won two gold medals at the U.S. Nationals and two medals at the Junior Worlds.

World Cup Arrival

In 2004, Lindsey won her first World Cup race with her downhill victory at Lake Louise in Alberta, Canada. She followed that sweet victory with five other podium finishes, and finished sixth overall in the world. Lindsey had arrived! At just 20, she was skiing and competing against the best **alpine** skiers in the entire world.

Lindsey battled strong winds and blowing snow as she skied to first place in Lake Louise.

She Said It

"Today I just tried to be relaxed...The weather was a little bit bad, but I hung in there and dealt with the conditions that were dealt to me and it seemed to go okay."
--Interview with Scott Russell, *CBC Sports*, in Lake Louise, December 3, 2004.

Red Bull Takes Over

Lindsey's training took a drastic turn when the beverage company and **sponsor** Red Bull came on board to train the U.S. Ski Team in 2005. The new coaches emphasized a wide variety of **cardio** and activity training geared toward strengthening the muscles used in skiing and increasing the team's **endurance**. They tailored training to each team member. Lindsey's specific fitness and physio training gradually built up her strength and speed. Lindsey says, "At first I would question every new suggestion. Gradually I saw my strength and performance improve, so my confidence in their training grew."

Once Red Bull took over, Lindsey wore a helmet that showed the new sponsor's logo.

14

Great Season

Lindsey's career saw immediate results after a few months of the Red Bull training regime. She won the downhill events in Lake Louise in Alberta, Canada, and at Val d'Isere, France. At the race in France, it is traditional to give the winner a cow! Lindsey keeps her unique prize on a friend's farm near the U.S. team's training hill in Austria.

Lindsey named the cow Olympe, no doubt because her next goal was the 2006 Olympics.

The Men in Her Life

Lindsey's love life got a boost when she started dating Thomas Vonn, a former Olympic skier. As Thomas and Lindsey's relationship grew closer, Lindsey and her father grew farther apart. Lindsey's father Alan didn't approve of his daughter dating someone who was nine years older than her. Her father's disapproval of Thomas, combined with his constant pressure on Lindsey to succeed, caused frequent major arguments between them. The added tension to their already strained relationship forced Lindsey to cut ties with her father. She no longer wanted him to be a part of her life.

15

Ski Sensation

Lindsey kept up with her rigorous training schedule and continued to dominate the slopes. Lindsey's dream was coming true—she was well on her way to becoming one of the greatest skiers in the entire world.

Olympic Spirit

In 2006, Lindsey competed in Turin, Italy, in her second Winter Olympics. She had the fastest time on the first training run but, on her second training run, she had a terrible crash. Lindsey spent just one night in hospital. The next day she got out and raced, in spite of her pain and bruises. She finished eighth overall, and her teammates awarded her the U.S. Olympic Spirit award for her bravery and determination.

Lindsey was taken off the mountain by helicopter after her crash in February 2006. Amazingly, Lindsey was only bruised and got back on the ski hill the next day!

Lindsey Wants to Win

Lindsey's coach Robert Trenkwalder says, "Lindsey is driven by winning." He says this is reflected in her high level of professionalism and her grueling training schedule. In the off-season, Lindsey often trains eight hours a day, six days a week. According to Trenkwalder, Lindsey "wants to give one hundred per cent, all of the time."

Here Comes the Bride

On top of her busy schedule, Lindsey made time to plan her wedding. Lindsey and Thomas decided to get married on September 29, 2007, at the Silver Lake Lodge in Deer Valley, Utah. Located on a mountain, it was the perfect place for two skiers to get married. Since Lindsey was not speaking with her father, she asked her grandfather to walk her down the aisle instead. Throughout their relationship, Thomas had become Lindsey's unofficial coach and mentor. He gave her helpful tips and also criticism, something many of her coaches were afraid to do. The pair had to learn how to keep their personal and professional lives separate. At times, they were coach and athlete, but they also had to remember to find time to be husband and wife.

Newly married couple Thomas and Lindsey Vonn

17

U.S. Men and Women on Top!

Lindsey finished off the 2007–2008 season by winning her first women's Overall World Cup Championship title. She was the second woman in U.S. history to do so. Her male teammate Bode Miller also won the men's Overall World Cup Championship title! That made the American skiers the best skiers in the world that year.

Lindsey with her U.S. Ski team teammate, Bode Miller

Not All Happy Times

Despite Lindsey's many achievements, behind the scenes she was fighting depression. She had felt the first symptoms of depression when her parents divorced, but instead of getting medical help, she had put all her energy and focus into skiing. But in 2008, despite having her best year ever on the hills, she was feeling unhappy much of the time. She sought treatment and was lucky to find medication that could help quickly. She went from struggling to get out of bed to truly enjoying her life again in a matter of a month.

Another Overall Win

Lindsey continued her domination on the slopes in the 2008–2009 season. She repeated her win of the Overall World Cup Championship and again won the downhill and Super-G championships.

Slope Domination

Unfortunately, the next season brought more injuries. In December 2009, during the opening run of the World Cup giant **slalom**, Lindsey crashed and nearly broke her arm. In true Lindsey style, she decided to work through the injury. Since her arm was just badly bruised, Lindsey continued to ski through the early winter months of 2010. She once again won the Overall World Cup Championship, as well as the downhill, Super-G, and combined categories for that season.

Even with her arm in a brace, she won three races in early January.

She Said It

"I know that I've worked harder and prepared myself better than anyone. And I have put things in place. I have a race routine. I have a team of people helping me. I have winning habits. I believe in myself. I have balance in my life. In the end, it's a mental maturity to let your best come out."
—*New York Times*, February 2010.

Olympic Dreams

The 2010 Winter Olympics in Vancouver, Canada, ran from February 12–28. Lindsey planned to compete in all five women's alpine ski events.

Unfortunately, just a few weeks before the Olympics, Lindsey badly bruised her shin. The injury made skiing at high speeds incredibly painful. But nothing was going to keep Lindsey from competing in the Olympics and she pressed on.

LAW & ORDER

Lindsey was not only on television during the Olympics in 2010, she also made a guest appearance on her favorite show, *Law & Order*. Lindsey played a secretary in the show's 20th season finale.

Olympic Gold!

Lindsey won a gold medal in her first event—downhill. She was the first American woman to ever win an Olympic gold medal for skiing. While she finished first in the downhill portion of the **super combined**, she missed a gate in the slalom portion and was disqualified. She won a bronze medal in the Super-G but, in the giant slalom, Lindsey missed a gate in heavy fog and crashed, breaking a finger. In the slalom, she lost control and straddled a gate and was disqualified. Despite the three races she did not finish, she won gold and bronze medals—an amazing accomplishment.

Lindsey became the unofficial skiing spokesperson at the 2010 Winter Olympics in Vancouver, Canada.

Just Missed in 2011

After three years of complete domination on the ski slopes, Lindsey lost the 2010–2011 Overall World Cup Championship to her friend and serious competitor Maria Riesch by just three points. Lindsey had suffered a concussion, or head injury, during this season and missed several races while she recovered.

Unhappy Ending

Injury wasn't the only difficulty Lindsey was facing in 2011. She was also suffering in her personal life. In November, Lindsey and Thomas announced that they had begun taking the steps to end their marriage. Lindsey felt that their marriage just wasn't working, and she decided she couldn't live with the unhappiness anymore. Their relationship had become more about work and less about love. Thomas would no longer be coaching or managing Lindsey's skiing career either.

LEARNING GERMAN

Lindsey and Maria Riesch are best friends. Lindsey learned to speak German by spending time at Maria's home in Germany.

Lindsey's fans love her. She was voted Favorite Female Athlete at Nickelodeon's 24th Annual Kids' Choice Awards in 2011.

21

Reconnecting with Dad

Lindsey reached out to her family for support while dealing with her divorce. This also included her father. She hadn't spoken with him in six years, but she decided to pick up the phone and tell him about her divorce. Lindsey had missed her father and wanted to try to rebuild their relationship. He helped her through her divorce and is now a part of her life again.

Back in 2012!

After her hard year in 2011, Lindsey came back better than ever. Not only did Lindsey win her fourth Overall World Cup Championship in 2012, but she also set several records and personal bests that year. She won her fifth Overall Downhill Championship, making it 25 downhill wins—the second most ever. She won all three races in Lake Louise, Alberta, for her second-ever career hat trick. Lindsey also won her 50th World Cup race in 2012.

Lindsey rounds a gate at Lake Louise, looking ahead to the next gate.

She Said It

"It's been a tough time in my life. It was time to let go. Family is complicated, but family is always family. It was just time. I wanted my dad back."
—Interview with *USA Today*.

Lindsey and Tiger

Lindsey's divorce from Thomas was final in January of 2013. A couple of months later, Lindsey announced that she was dating golf star Tiger Woods. The two met at a charity event in April 2012 and Lindsey says they "immediately clicked." They maintained a long-distance friendship but, by the fall, it had become more serious. Lindsey admits that it was strange to be with Tiger at first because he is always followed around by the media, but she says it's worth it.

Lindsey and Tiger take his children, Sam, age 6, and Charlie, age 4, out on jet skis during a holiday weekend.

Victory After a Partial Season

In February 2013, Lindsey had a horrible crash during the Super-G race in the Alpine World Championships. She was airlifted to hospital where she had to undergo major knee surgery. The crash ended her season, but Lindsey had built up enough points early in the season to win her sixth downhill World Cup Championship. For only racing for part of the season, this was an amazing accomplishment. Lindsey left the season vowing she would beat the injury and be back for the 2014 Winter Olympics in Sochi, Russia.

Off the Slopes

Despite Lindsey's busy training and racing schedules, she devotes a lot of time to a variety of causes off the ski hill and is frequently spotted at events. She has become a busy spokesperson for her sport and a famous face. She uses her fame to help others, particularly those who have suffered the types of injuries that skiers sometimes suffer. Lindsey's beautiful face and friendly spirit also make her a favorite at red carpet events where she is often photographed.

Lindsey walks the red carpet at the 2012 ESPY Awards in Los Angeles.

Giving Back

Lindsey supports a charity called Wings for Life, whose goal is to make spinal cord injuries curable. The organization supports research projects targeting the repair of spinal cord injuries, many of which lead to paralysis, or the inability to move, in legs or other limbs. Given the nature of injuries in downhill skiing, Lindsey is sensitive to those who suffer such injuries. Wings for Life was also started by the founder of Red Bull, one of Lindsey's main sponsors.

Supporting Wounded Veterans

Lindsey also supports the Wounded Warrior Project. This organization supports wounded U.S. Army veterans as they come home and have to get used to being civilians, or non-soldiers, again. Not only have these men and women come back from a war zone, but many have also come back with injuries that have changed their lives. The Wounded Warrior Project organizes events and long-term programs for these veterans. It also introduces them to other veterans who have already made the transition back into civilian life so they feel less alone.

Lindsey attends the 17th Annual Race to Erase MS—a benefit to help raise money for Multiple Sclerosis research.

SKIER TURNED SINGER

During the Race to Erase MS benefit, Lindsey joined singer Avril Lavigne and others on stage to sing the famous song "Lean on Me" by Bill Withers.

She Said It

"[Lindsey's] real and she's cool. She's the most down-to-earth girl. And she's been through a lot. But at a certain point in your life you realize what your priorities should be, and I think she has gotten there."
—Cynthia Rowley, discussing her friend Lindsey Vonn in a *Vogue* magazine article from July 2013

Sponsorships

Lindsey's good looks and success as a skier has made her a favorite for ski supplier sponsorships. For most of her career, Lindsey raced on Rossignol skis and had a full sponsorship with that company. In 2009, Lindsey changed her sponsor to Head. Lindsey also has sponsorship deals with sportswear company Under Armour, sunglass and clothing brand Oakley, and Rolex watch company.

Professional athletes often have marketing deals with more than one sponsor. The sponsor usually requires the athlete to display their company logo on the athlete's clothing when they compete.

Energy Drinks

Lindsey is also sponsored by Red Bull, a company that produces energy drinks. There is much debate about the health effects of energy drinks. Marketed as short-term energy boosters, the drinks' ingredients increase heart rate and blood pressure. Energy drinks are often banned in schools because of this.

Lindsey's Smile

Lindsey is widely recognized for her friendly smile and all around good looks. She was a model spokesperson for downhill skiing at the 2010 Winter Olympics in Vancouver, Canada, where she won gold in the downhill event. Lindsey has appeared in several magazines recognizing Olympians and Lindsey's all around achievements. *Sports Illustrated* has published a number of cover and inside shots of her in their magazines. Some people didn't agree with a few pictures of Lindsey in a bathing suit for their swimsuit issue, and a cover shot on a preview issue for the Olympics, however. Some thought these pictures made Lindsey look too sexy and didn't show her as a serious athlete.

SPRING TRAINING 2010
The Unlikely Genius Behind the New Moneyba
By ALBERT CHEN

MARCH 1, 2010

Sports Illustrated

FAST COMPANY
By TIM LAYDEN

AMERICAN AMPLITUDE
By AUSTIN MURPHY

U.S. racers Andrew Weibrecht, Lindsey Vonn, Bode Miller and Julia Mancuso with their record medal hau Alpine skiing

Lindsey appears on a *Sports Illustrated* cover showing the U.S. skiing medalists from the 2010 Vancouver Winter Olympics.

Men vs. Women?

In 2012, Lindsey approached the International Ski Federation (FIS) with a request to allow her to ski against the men on the tour. FIS rules do not allow skiers of one gender to compete in races of the other gender. Her request was denied, but Lindsey vows to continue to keep trying. She has trained with male skiers and has even posted faster times than some of the men. She would now like to try competing against them.

Long-term Vision

Long term, Lindsey sees herself skiing through to the 2018 Olympics. She has said that if she were to retire then, at the age of 33, this could be a good time to make a change. Of course all this will depend on her staying healthy and happy on the slopes from now until then. Eventually, she sees herself wanting to start a family and spending more time at home in one place. Lindsey is also interested in possibly pursuing a career in acting.

Lindsey proudly wears the dress her friend, designer Cynthia Rowley, made for the CFDA Fashion Awards.

28

Timeline

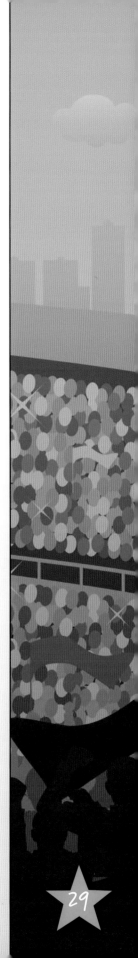

1984: Lindsey Caroline Kildow is born in St. Paul, Minnesota

1991: Lindsey is inspired when she meets U.S. Olympic gold medal ski racer Picabo Street

1999: Became the first American to ever win an important race in Italy called the Trofeo Topolino

2002: Competes in her first Olympics and places 6th in the combined event

2005: Competes at her first World Championship in Italy and places 4th and 9th.

2005: Red Bull joins the U.S. Ski Team and takes over Lindsey's training program

2006: Crashes in a training run at the Winter Olympics but races anyway and places 8th

2007: Marries U.S. Ski Team athlete Thomas Vonn on September 29

2008: Wins the Overall Women's World Cup Championship

2008: Diagnosed with depression

2009: Wins the Overall Women's World Cup Championship

2010: Wins the Overall Women's World Cup Championship

2010: Makes a guest appearance on *Law & Order*

2011: Files for divorce from husband Thomas

2011: Wins a gold medal for downhill at the Vancouver Winter Olympics and bronze for Super-G

2012: Wins the Overall Women's World Cup Championship

2013: Lindsey and Tiger Woods announce in March they are dating

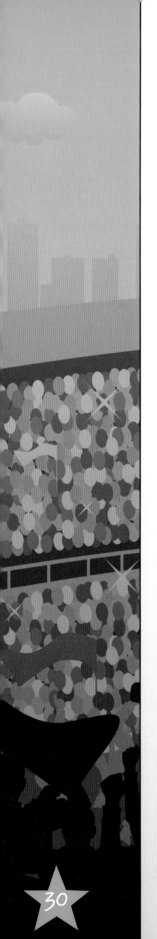

Glossary

alpine Refers to something that takes place in high mountains including the Alps

cardio Short for "cardiovascular," which relates to the heart and blood vessels

combined A race that includes both a slalom and a downhill course

downhill The fastest speed race in alpine ski racing where skiers ski around gates or flags that are set far apart on a steep mountain slope

endurance The ability to withstand physical challenges for a long time

fall line The line down a mountain that goes most directly downhill

Overall World Cup Championship The trophy awarded at the end of each ski season to the alpine ski racer who has the most points from World Cup events in all categories

perseverance Working at something without giving up

podium Place where the first-, second-, and third-place prizes or medals are awarded

prestigious Something that has a reputation and is highly regarded due to past achievements

slalom Downhill skiing courses with gates set close together, requiring skiers to make tight turns at fast speeds to get through the gates

sponsor A person or company who supports someone else in return for that person's promotion of their product

stroke A medical condition limiting blood flow to the brain, causing permanent or temporary brain damage, the inability to move arms or legs, or even death

super combined A ski course that has both a slalom and a shortened Super-G course

Super-G Short for Super Giant Slalom

Find Out More

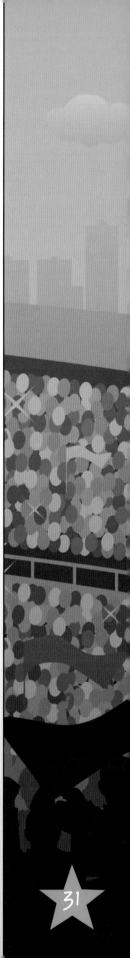

Books

Tieck, Sarah. *Lindsey Vonn: Olympic Champion*. Big
    Buddy Books, ABDO Publishing Company, 2011.

Gitlin, Marty. *Lindsey Vonn*. Lucent Books, 2012

Websites

Lindsy Vonn
    www.lindseyvonn.com
Lindsey Vonn's official website features photos,
details about her career, video of her skiing, details
about her charities, and links to her facebook and
twitter pages.

Wings for Life
    www.wingsforlife.com
Wings for Life is a charity Lindsey actively supports.
This group helps to fund research that is looking for
a cure for spinal cord injury.

Index

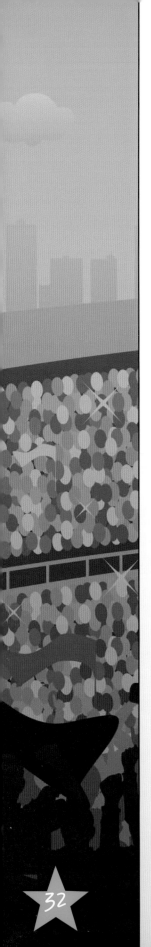

About the Author

Sarah Dann publishes her own magazine and writes a variety of articles for various publications. She attended university to perfect her writing skills by studying English and Journalism. Sarah has written several titles and found the Superstars! series to be particularly inspiring with their message of working hard to get amazing results.